THE PHILLIP KEVEREN SERIES EASY PIANO

LIVING HOPE

15 CONTEMPORARY WORSHIP SONGS

Arranged by Phillip Keveren

— PIANO LEVEL —
EARLY INTERMEDIATE

ISBN 978-1-70511-101-7

HAL•LEONARD®

Visit Hal Leonard Online at
www.halleonard.com

Visit Phillip at
www.phillipkeveren.com

Contact us:
Hal Leonard
7777 West Bluemound Road
Milwaukee, WI 53213
Email: info@halleonard.com

In Europe, contact:
Hal Leonard Europe Limited
42 Wigmore Street
Marylebone, London, W1U 2RN
Email: info@halleonardeurope.com

In Australia, contact:
Hal Leonard Australia Pty. Ltd.
4 Lentara Court
Cheltenham, Victoria, 3192 Australia
Email: info@halleonard.com.au

PREFACE

We are pleased to present this collection of current worship songs, carefully prepared for Easy Piano. It is our hope that these arrangements will provide playable, full-sounding settings for private worship at the piano, church services, or recitals.

The Lord bless you and keep you, make His face to shine upon you...

Phillip Keveren

BIOGRAPHY

Phillip Keveren, a multi-talented keyboard artist and composer, has composed original works in a variety of genres from piano solo to symphonic orchestra. He gives frequent concerts and workshops for teachers and their students in the United States, Canada, Europe, and Asia. Mr. Keveren holds a B.M. in composition from California State University Northridge and a M.M. in composition from the University of Southern California.

CONTENTS

THE BLESSING

Words and Music by KARI JOBE CARNES,
CODY CARNES, STEVEN FURTICK
and CHRIS BROWN
Arranged by Phillip Keveren

Joyfully (♩ = 69)

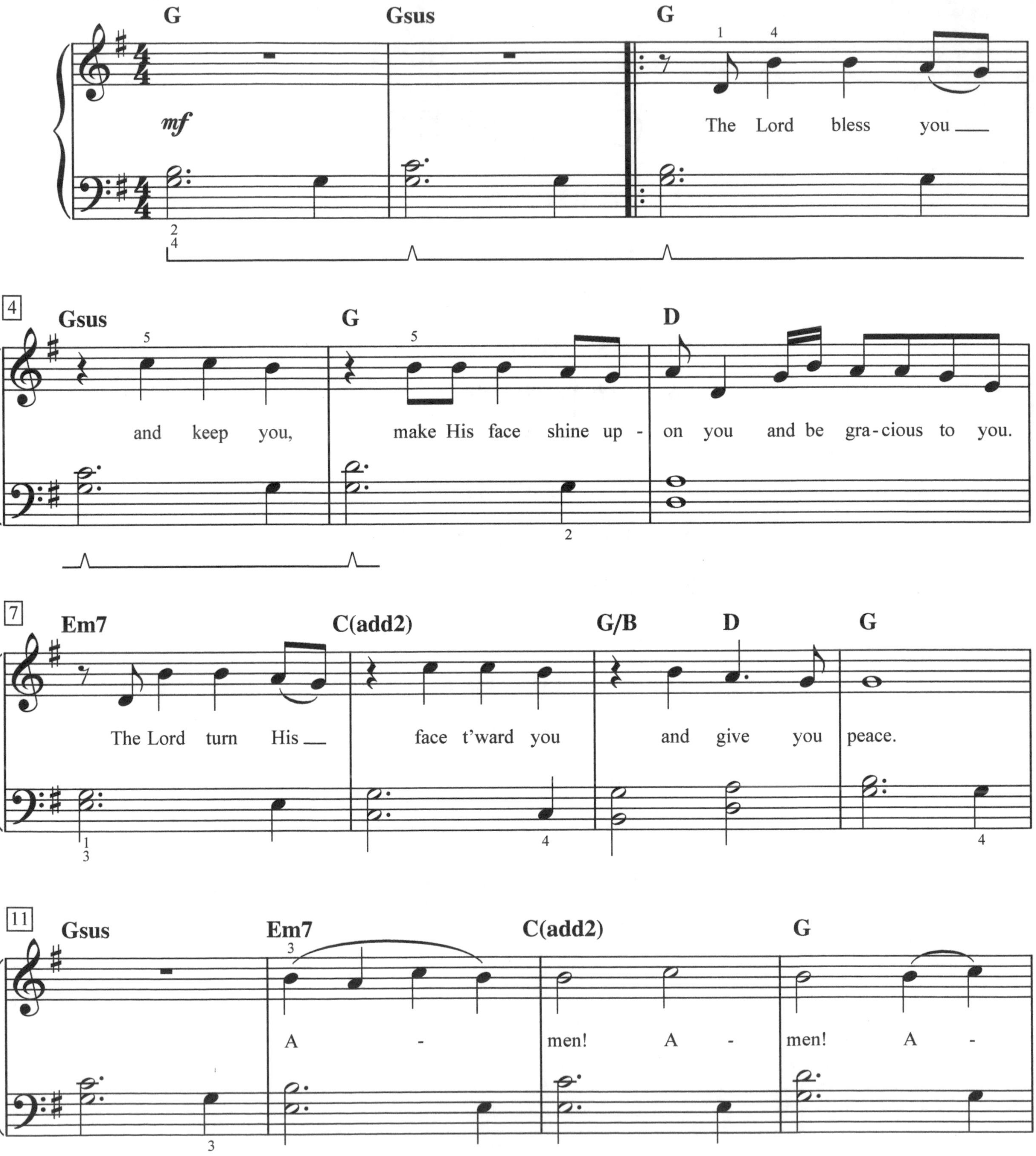

15
D
Em7
C(add2)
G
men! A - men! A - men! A -
19
1.
2.
D
D
Em7
men! men! May His fa - vor be up - on ___ you, and a
22
C(add2)
G
thou - sand gen - er - a - tions, and your fam - 'ly, and their chil - dren, and their
24
D
Em7
chil - dren, and their chil - dren. May His pres - ence go be - fore ___ you, and be -

26
C(add2)
G
hind you, and in - side ___ you, all a - round you, and with - in ___ you. He is
28
D
Em7
with you, He is with ___ you, in the morn - ing, in the eve - ning, in your
30
C(add2)
G
com - ing and your go - ing, in your weep - ing and re - joic - ing. He is
32
D
Em7
for you, He is for ___ you, He is for you, He is for ___ you, He is

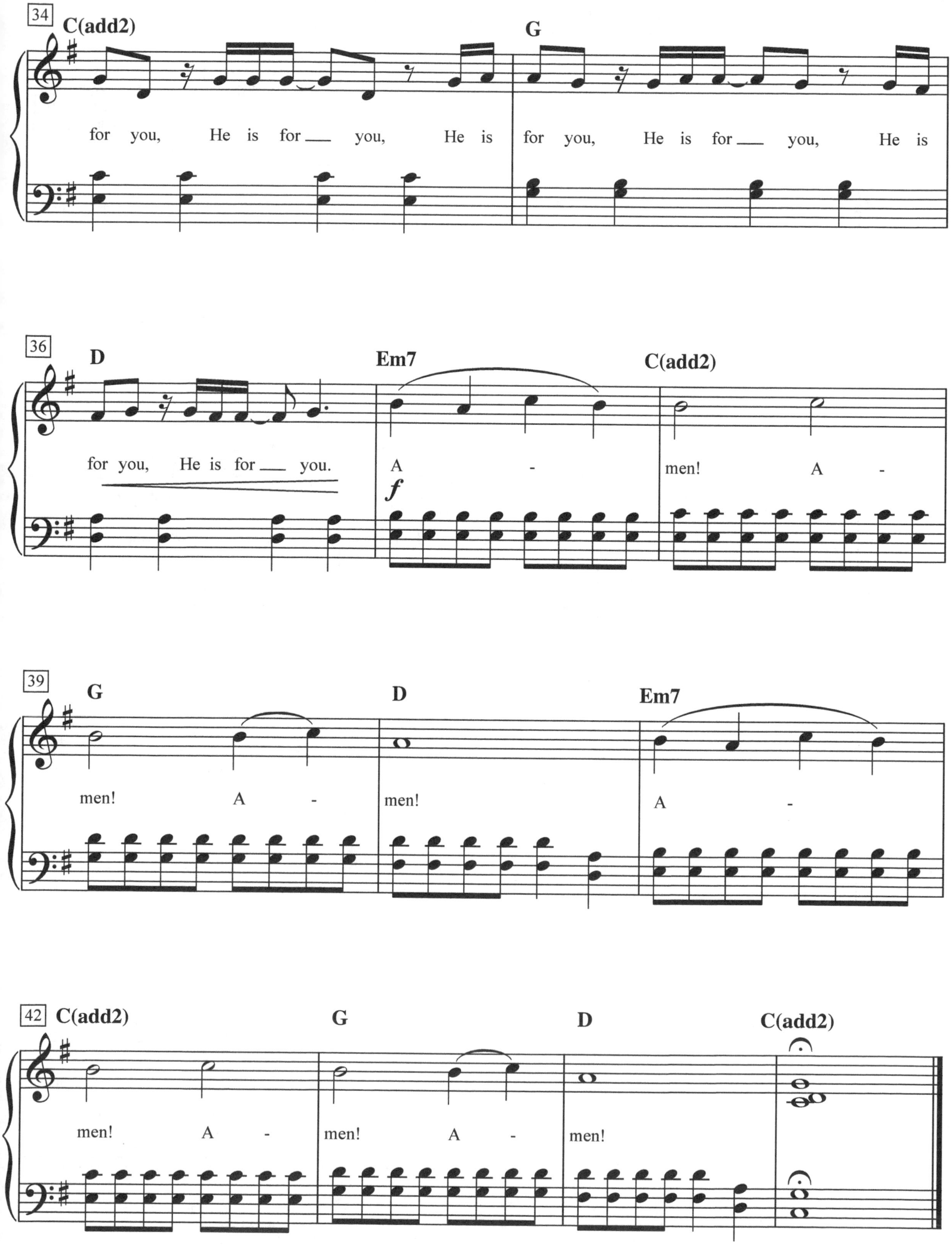
34
C(add2)
G
for you, He is for you, He is for you, He is for you, He is
36
D
Em7
C(add2)
for you, He is for you. A - men! A -
f
39
G
D
Em7
men! A - men! A -
42
C(add2)
G
D
C(add2)
men! A - men! A - men!

BUILD MY LIFE

Words and Music by MATT REDMAN,
PAT BARRETT, BRETT YOUNKER,
KARL MARTIN and KIRBY KAPLE
Arranged by Phillip Keveren

Moderately slow (♩ = 72)

12
C
G
C
bove ev-'ry oth-er name.
Je - sus, the on - ly
one who would ev-er save.
15
G
C
Wor - thy of ev - 'ry
breath we could ev - er breathe,
we live for
17
G
C(add2)
You,
oh, we live for
You.
Ho - ly, there is no one
20
Am7
G/D
Em7
like You, there is none be - side You.
O - pen up my
eyes in won - der, and

23
C(add2)
Am7
G/D
show me who You are, and fill me with Your heart, and lead me in Your love to
26
Em7
C(add2)
G/D
Em7
those a - round me.
30
G/B
C(add2)
G/D
Em7
4
I will build my life up - on Your love. It is a
34
G/B
C(add2)
G/D
firm foun - da - tion. I will put my trust in You a -

37
Em7
G/B
C(add2)
lone, and I will not be shak - en. Ho - ly, there is no one
40
Am7
G/D
Em7
like You, there is none be - side You. O - pen up my eyes in won - der, and
43
C(add2)
Am7
G/D
show me who You are, and fill me with Your heart, and lead me in Your love to
46
Em7
C(add2)
those a - round me.

HOLY SPIRIT

Words and Music by KATIE TORWALT
and BRYAN TORWALT
Arranged by Phillip Keveren

10
B♭maj7
Your pres - ence,
Lord.
13
F
B♭maj7
I've tast - ed and seen
of the sweet-est of loves,
where my heart be-comes free
16
F
and my shame is un - done.
Your pres - ence,
19
B♭maj7
Lord.
F
Ho - ly Spir - it, You are

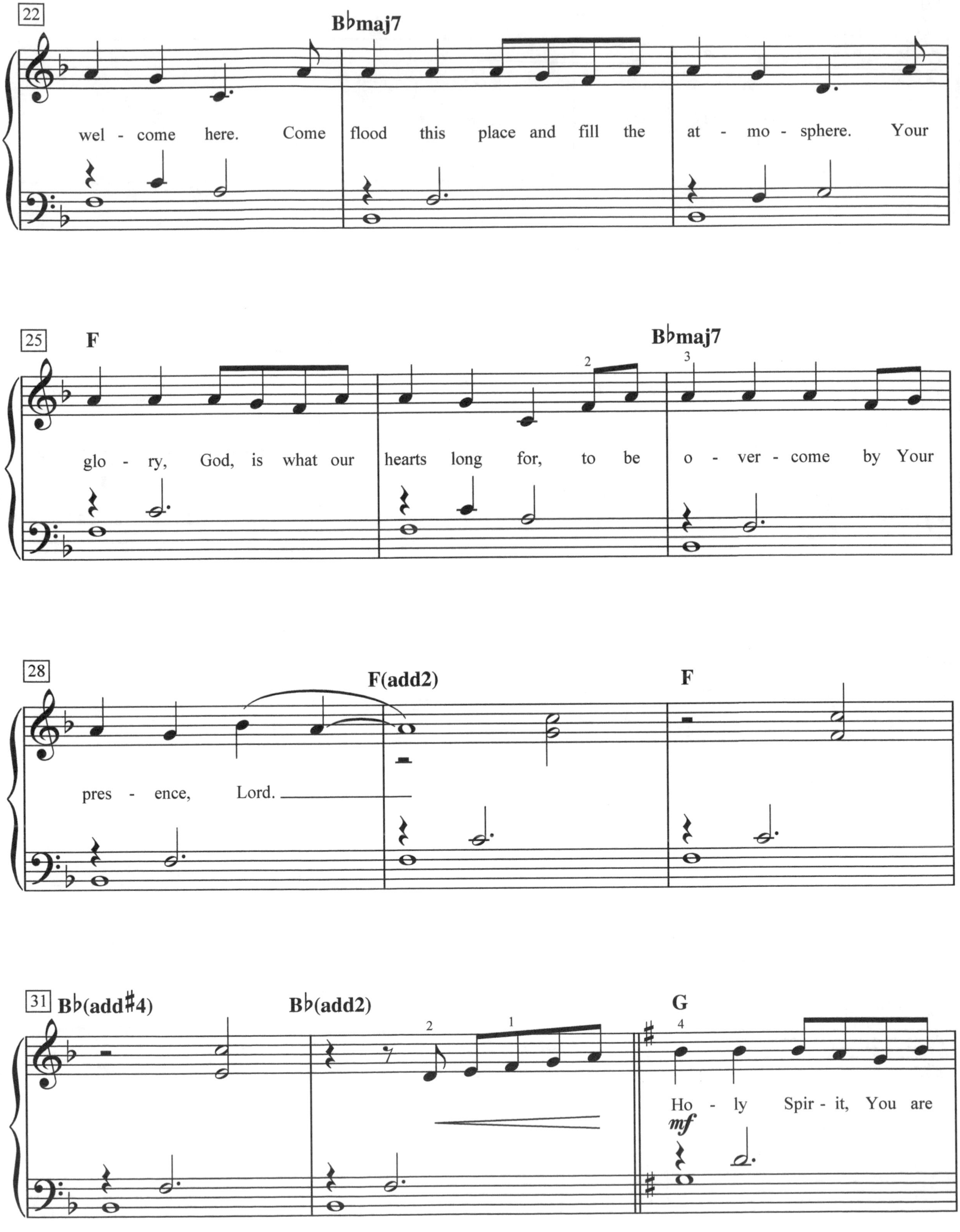
22
B♭maj7
wel - come here. Come flood this place and fill the at - mo - sphere. Your
25
F
B♭maj7
glo - ry, God, is what our hearts long for, to be o - ver - come by Your
28
F(add2)
F
pres - ence, Lord.
31
B♭(add♯4)
B♭(add2)
G
Ho - ly Spir - it, You are
mf

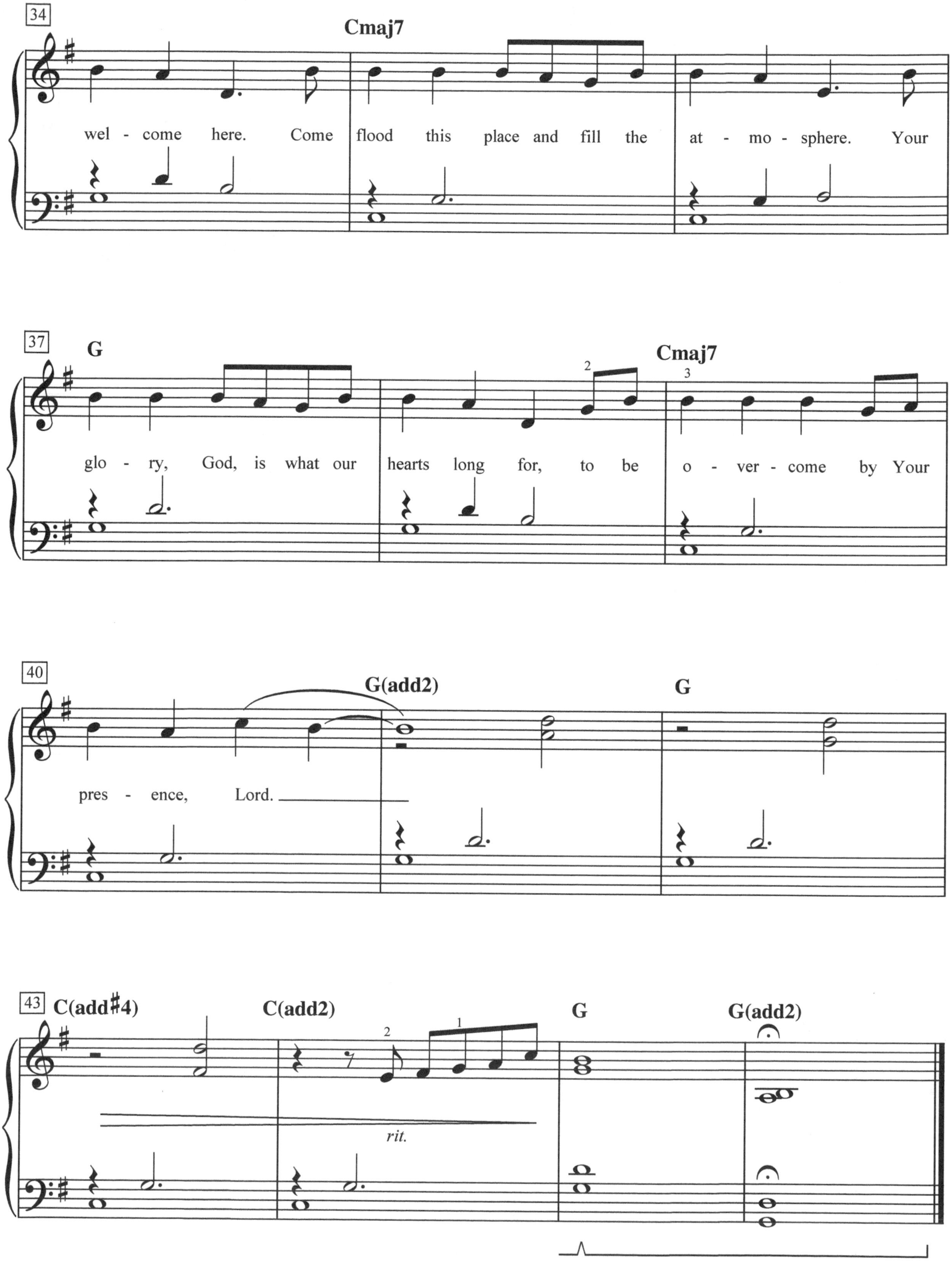
34
Cmaj7
wel - come here. Come flood this place and fill the at - mo - sphere. Your
37
G
Cmaj7
glo - ry, God, is what our hearts long for, to be o - ver - come by Your
40
G(add2)
G
pres - ence, Lord.
43
C(add♯4)
C(add2)
G
G(add2)
rit.

IS HE WORTHY?

Words and Music by ANDREW PETERSON
and BEN SHIVE
Arranged by Phillip Keveren

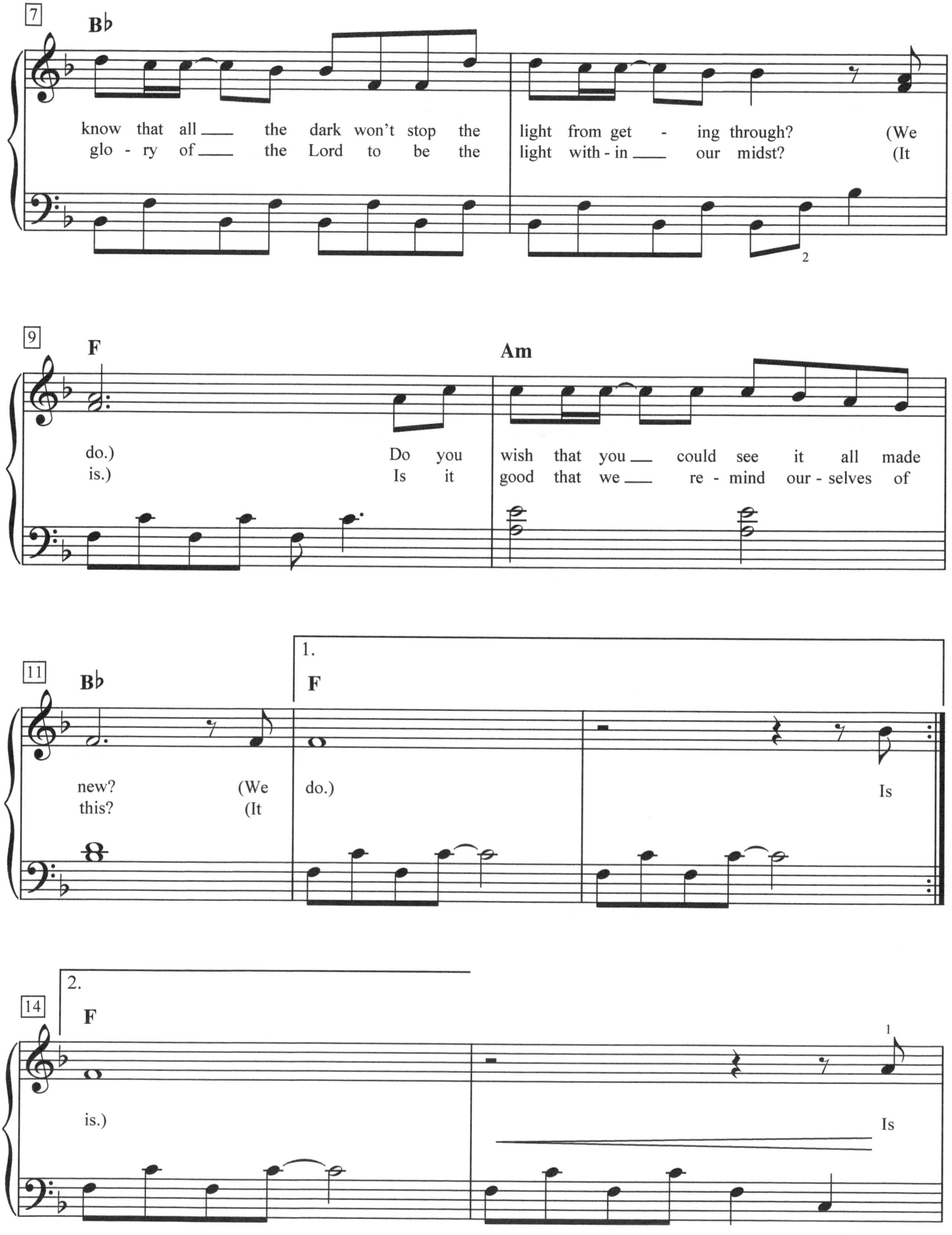
7
B♭
know that all the dark won't stop the light from get - ing through? (We
glo - ry of the Lord to be the light with - in our midst? (It
2
9
F
Am
do.) Do you wish that you could see it all made
is.) Is it good that we re - mind our - selves of
11
B♭
1.
F
new? (We do.) Is
this? (It
2.
14
F
1
is.) Is

16
B♭
C
an - y - one wor - thy? Is an - y - one whole? Is
mf
18
Dm
C
B♭
an - y - one a - ble to break the seal and o - pen the scroll? The
20
C
Li - on of Ju - dah who con-quered the grave, He is
22
Dm
C
To Coda
B♭
Da - vid's root and the Lamb who died to ran-som the slave. Is He

24
Dm C F/A B♭ Dm C
wor - thy? Is He wor - thy of all bless-ing and hon - or and
27
F/A B♭ Dm C B♭
glo - ry? Is He wor - thy of this? He
30
F
is.
mp
Does the Fa - ther tru - ly love us? (He
33
Dm7
does.) Does the Spir - it move _ a - mong us? (He does.) And does

36
B♭
Je - sus, our Mes - si - ah, hold for - ev - er those He loves? (He
38
F
Am
B♭
does.) Does our God in - tend to dwell with us a - gain? (He
41
F
D.S. al Coda
does.) Is
CODA
B♭
ran-som the slave. From ev - 'ry
f
43
B♭/D
C/E
peo - ple and tribe, ev - 'ry na - tion and tongue, He has

45
F
F/A
B♭
made us a king-dom and priests to God to reign with the Son. Is He
47
Dm
C
F/A
B♭
Dm
C
wor - thy? Is He wor - thy of all bless-ing and hon-or and
50
F/A
B♭
Dm
C
F/A
B♭
glo - ry? Is He wor - thy? Is He wor - thy? Is He
53
Dm
C
B♭
C7sus
F
wor - thy of this? He is.
rit.

KING OF KINGS

Words and Music by SCOTT LIGERTWOOD,
BROOKE LIGERTWOOD and JASON INGRAM
Arranged by Phillip Keveren

Moderately (♩ = 88)

13
D G Bm7
Praise the Fa - ther, praise the Son, praise the Spir - it,
f
16
D/A A D G
Three in One. God of glo - ry, maj - es - ty,
19
Bm7 Gmaj7 A7
1.
D Dsus
praise for - ev - er to the King of kings.
To re -
mf
23
2.
D Dsus D
kings.

KING OF MY HEART

Words and Music by JOHN MARK McMILLAN
and SARAH McMILLAN
Arranged by Phillip Keveren

13
Dm F/C B♭ F Dm F/C
good, good, oh. You are good, good,
16
B♭ F Dm F/C
1.
B♭ F
oh. You are good, good, oh. Let the
2.
19
B♭ F
oh. You're nev-er gon-na let, nev-er gon-na let me down.
22
Dm7 F
You're nev-er gon-na let, nev-er gon-na let me down. You're nev-er gon-na let,

25
Dm7 F/C Bb(add2) Csus
nev-er gon-na let me down.
You're nev-er gon-na let,
nev-er gon-na let me down. You are
28
Dm F/C Bb F Dm F/C
good, good,
oh. You are
good, good,
31
Bb F Dm F/C Bb F
oh. You are
good, good,
oh. You are
34
Dm F/C Bb F
good, good,
oh.

HIS MERCY IS MORE

Words and Music by MATT BOSWELL
and MATT PAPA
Arranged by Phillip Keveren

Slow Gospel feel (♩. = 48)

13
F Bb F C Dm7
love could re - mem - ber no wrongs we have done? Om - ni - scient, all - know - ing, He
pa - tience would wait as we con - stant - ly roam? What Fa - ther so ten - der is
rich - es of kind - ness He lav - ished on us! His blood was the pay - ment, His
16
Bb C F Gm7 F/A
counts not their sum, thrown in - to a sea with - out bot - tom or
call - ing us home? He wel - comes the weak - est, the vil - est, the
life was the cost. We stood 'neath a debt we could nev - er af -
19
Bb F/A Bb F C
shore. Our sins, they are man - y; His mer - cy is
poor. Our sins, they are man - y; His mer - cy is
ford. Our sins, they are man - y; His mer - cy was
22
F Bb F Dm7 C
more. more. more. Praise the Lord, His mer - cy is

25
B♭ F C B♭ F
more.
Strong - er than dark - ness,
28
C Dm B♭ F C
new ev - 'ry morn. Our sins, they are man - y; His mer - cy is
31
F B♭ F
more.
34
1., 2.
B♭
What
What
3.
B♭ F
rit.

THE LION AND THE LAMB

Words and Music by BRENTON BROWN,
BRIAN JOHNSON and LEELAND MOORING
Arranged by Phillip Keveren

11
F
f
Our God is the Li - on, the Li - on of
13
Dm
Ju - dah, He's roar - ing with pow - er and fight - ing our
15
B♭
C
bat - tles. And ev - 'ry knee will bow be - fore Him.
17
F
Our God is the Lamb, the Lamb that was

19
Dm
slain for the sin of the world. His blood breaks the
21
B♭
C
chains, and ev - 'ry knee will bow be - fore the Li - on and the
23
B♭
C
Lamb. Oh, ev - 'ry knee will bow be - fore the Li - on and the
25
F
Gm
To Coda
B♭
Lamb.

28
Gm
F/A
p
Who can stop the Lord Al - might - y?
31
B♭
C
Gm
Who can stop the Lord Al - might - y?
cresc.
Who can stop the
34
F/A
B♭
C
D.S. al Coda
Lord Al - might - y?
Who can stop the Lord?
CODA
B♭
F5
rit.

LIVING HOPE

Words and Music by PHIL WICKHAM
and BRIAN JOHNSON
Arranged by Phillip Keveren

14
C Am Gsus C
kind - ness _ tore through the shad - ows of my soul. The work is fin - ished, _ the end is
18
G F Gsus C F C
writ - ten. Je - sus Christ, my liv - ing hope. Hal - le - lu - jah! Praise the
f
22
G Am F C G Am G
One who set me free. Hal - le - lu - jah! Death has lost its grip on me. You have
25
F C G Am F Gsus G
bro - ken ev - 'ry chain, there's sal - va - tion in Your name. Je - sus Christ, my liv - ing

28
C F C
hope. Hal - le - lu - jah! Praise the
30
G Am F C
One who set me free. Hal - le - lu - jah! Death has
32
G Am F C
lost its grip on me. You have bro - ken ev - 'ry chain, there's sal -
34
G Am F Gsus G C
va - tion in Your name. Je - sus Christ, my liv - ing hope.
rit.

LORD, I NEED YOU

Words and Music by JESSE REEVES,
KRISTIAN STANFILL, MATT MAHER,
CHRISTY NOCKELS and DANIEL CARSON
Arranged by Phillip Keveren

14
Em C/E G/D D G C G C
ev - 'ry hour I need You. My one de-fense, my right - eous-ness; oh,
18
G/D D G C G C G D Em
God how I need You. So teach my song to rise to You
p
22
C D C G D
when temp - ta - tion comes my way. When I can - not stand, I'll fall on
25
Em C D G Cm E♭/F
You. Je- sus, You're my hope and stay. Lord, I
cresc.

29
B♭ E♭ B♭ F Gm E♭/G
need You, oh, I need You; ev - 'ry hour I
f
32
B♭/F F B♭/D Cm/E♭ B♭/F E♭/G
need You. My one de-fense, my right - eous-ness; oh,
35
B♭/F F7 B♭ B♭/D Cm/E♭
God, how I need You. You're my one de-fense, my
mf
38
B♭/F E♭/G B♭/F F7 B♭
right - eous-ness; oh, God, how I need You.
dim. e rit.
p

RAISE A HALLELUJAH

Words and Music by JONATHAN DAVID HELSER,
MELISSA HELSER, MOLLY SKAGGS
and JAKE STEVENS
Arranged by Phillip Keveren

13
Dsus
D
weap - on is a mel - o - dy.
I
raise a hal - le - lu - jah;
16
Dsus
heav - en comes to fight for me.
19
G
D
I'm gon - na sing in the mid-dle of the storm.
21
Bm
Asus
Loud - er and loud - er, you're gon-na hear my prais - es roar.

23
G
D
Bm
To Coda
Up from the ash - es, hope will a - rise. Death is de - feat - ed, the
26
Asus
D
King is a - live. I raise a hal - le - lu - jah
29
G
3
2
with ev - 'ry-thing in - side of me. I
32
Bm
Asus
2
raise a hal - le - lu - jah; I will watch the dark-ness flee.

35
D
I raise a hal - le - lu - jah in the
38
G
Bm
mid - dle of the mys - ter - y.
I raise a hal - le - lu - jah;
41
Asus
D.S. al Coda
fear, you lost your grip on me.
CODA
Asus
King is a - live.

46
D
Sing a lit-tle loud - er in the pres - ence of my en - e - mies.
48
Asus
Sing a lit-tle loud - er, loud - er than my un - be - lief.
50
Bm7
Sing a lit-tle loud - er; my weap - on is a mel - o - dy.
52
G
Sing a lit-tle loud - er; heav - en comes to fight for me.

54
G
D
Sing a lit-tle loud - er; I'm gon - na sing in the mid-dle of the storm.
57
Bm
Asus
A
Loud - er and loud - er, you're gon-na hear my prais - es roar.
59
G
D
Bm
Up from the ash - es, hope will a - rise. Death is de - feat - ed, the
62
Asus
D
King is a - live.
rit.

WAY MAKER

Words and Music by
OSINACHI OKORO
Arranged by Phillip Keveren

With reverence (♩ = 69)

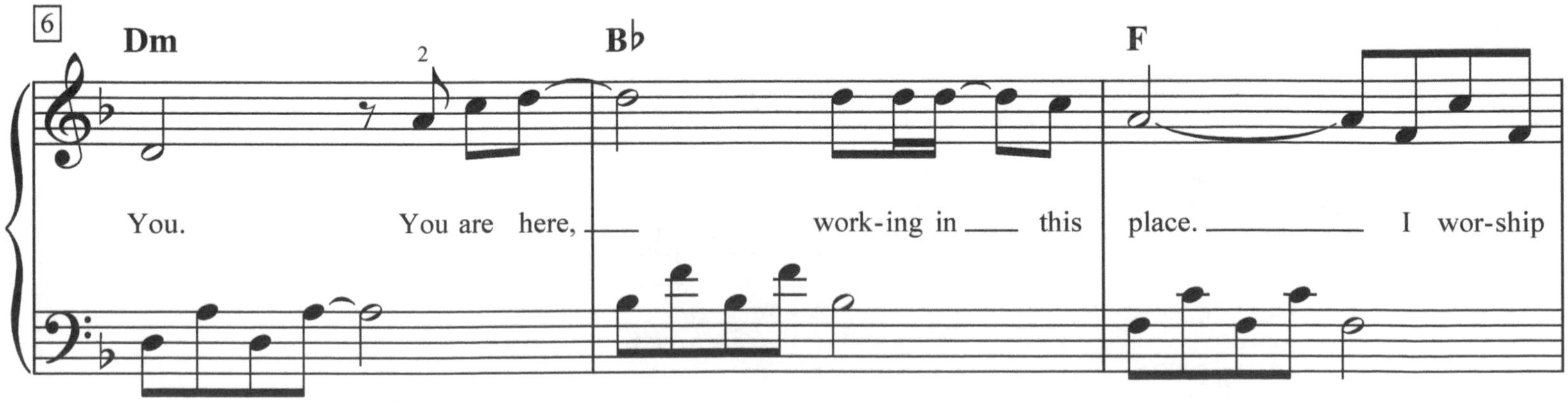

9
C
1.
Dm F/A
2.
Dm C/E F
You, I wor-ship You. You are here, You.
12
B♭
F
mf Way mak-er, mir-a-cle work-er, prom-ise keep-er, light in the dark-ness,
14
C
Dm F/A B♭
my God, that is who You are. Way mak-er, mir-a-cle work-er,
17
F
C
Dm F/A
prom-ise keep-er, light in the dark-ness, my God, that is who You are. You are here,
mp

20
B♭
F
C
touch-ing ev - 'ry heart. I wor-ship You, I wor-ship
turn-ing lives a - round. I wor-ship You, I wor-ship
23
Dm
B♭
F
You. You are here, heal-ing ev - 'ry heart. I wor-ship
You. You are here, mend-ing ev - 'ry heart. I wor-ship
26
C
1.
Dm
F/A
2.
Dm
C/E
F
You, I wor-ship You. You are here,
You, I wor-ship You.
29
B♭
F
C
mf
Way mak-er, mir-a-cle work-er, prom-ise keep-er, light in the dark-ness, my God, that is who You

32
Dm F/A B♭ F
are. Way mak-er, mir-a-cle work er, prom-ise keep-er, light in the dark-ness,
35
C Dm F/A B♭
my God, that is who You are. You are here, touch-ing ev - 'ry
mp
38
F C Dm
life. I wor-ship You, I wor-ship You. You are here,
41
B♭ F C Dm
meet-ing ev - 'ry need. I wor-ship You, I wor-ship You.
rit.

RECKLESS LOVE

Words and Music by CALEB CULVER,
CORY ASBURY and RAN JACKSON
Arranged by Phillip Keveren

Flowing (♩. = 52)

10
Em
D
Be-fore I took a breath, You breathed Your
When I felt no worth, You paid all
13
C(add2)
Em
life in me.
for me.
You have been
You have been
16
D
C(add2)
so, so good to me.
so, so good to me.
Oh, the
f
19
Em
D
C(add2)
G
o - ver - whelm - ing, nev - er - end - ing, reck - less love of God. Oh, it

23
Em
D
C(add2)
chas - es me down, fights till I'm found, leaves the nine - ty -
26
G
Em7
D
nine. I could - n't earn it, and I don't de - serve it, still You
29
C(add2)
G
Em
D
give Your - self a - way. Oh, the o - ver - whelm - ing, nev - er - end - ing,
1.
2.
33
C(add2)
G
C(add2)
G
reck - less love of God.
reck - less love of God.

WHAT A BEAUTIFUL NAME

Words and Music by BEN FIELDING
and BROOKE LIGERTWOOD
Arranged by Phillip Keveren

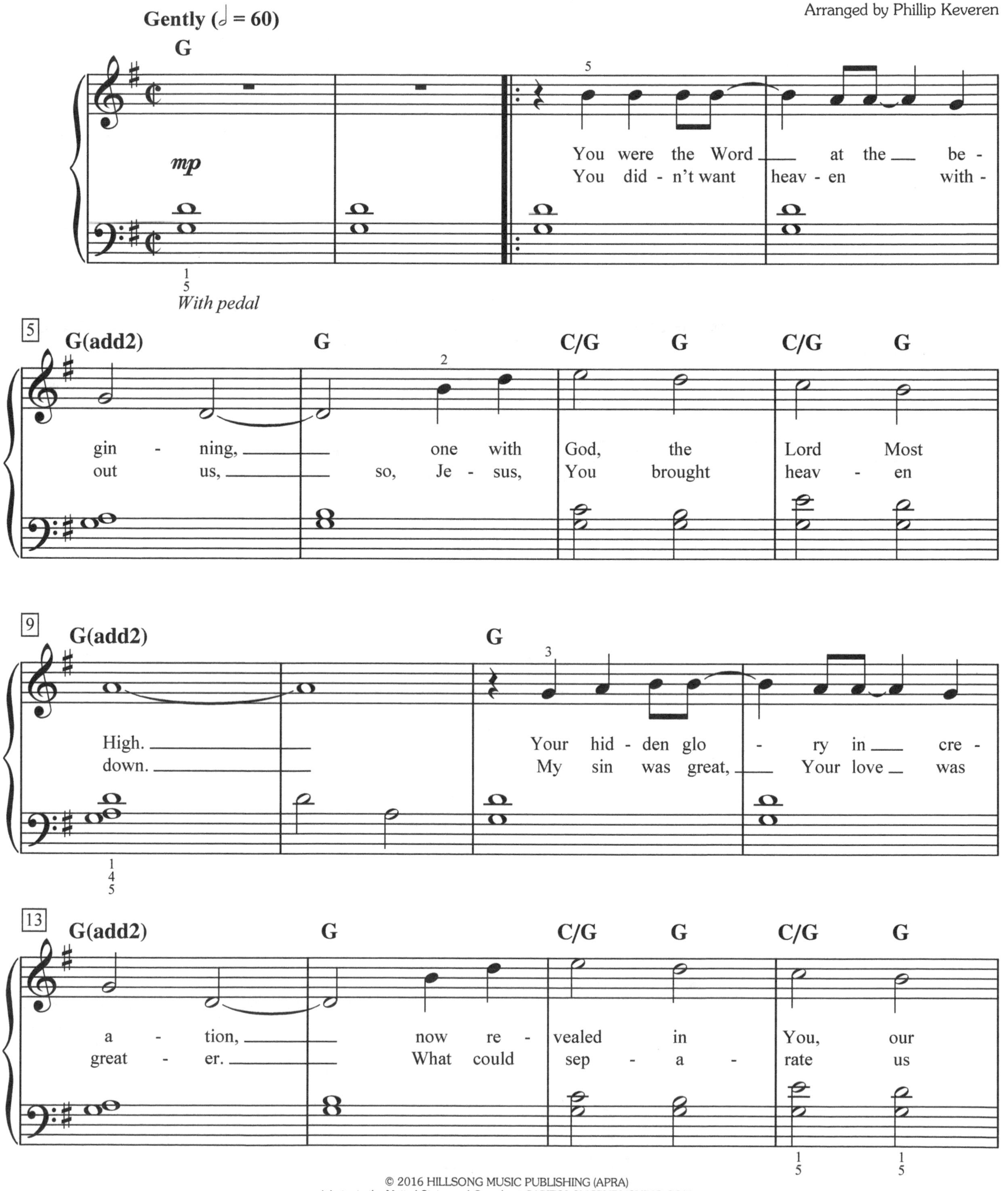

17
D/F#
G
Christ. now? What a beau - ti - ful name it is, what a
20
D/F#
Em7
beau - ti - ful name it is, the name of Je - sus Christ,
24
D/F#
C/G
G
my King. What a beau - ti - ful name it is,
28
D/F#
noth - ing com - pares to this. What a beau - ti - ful name it is,

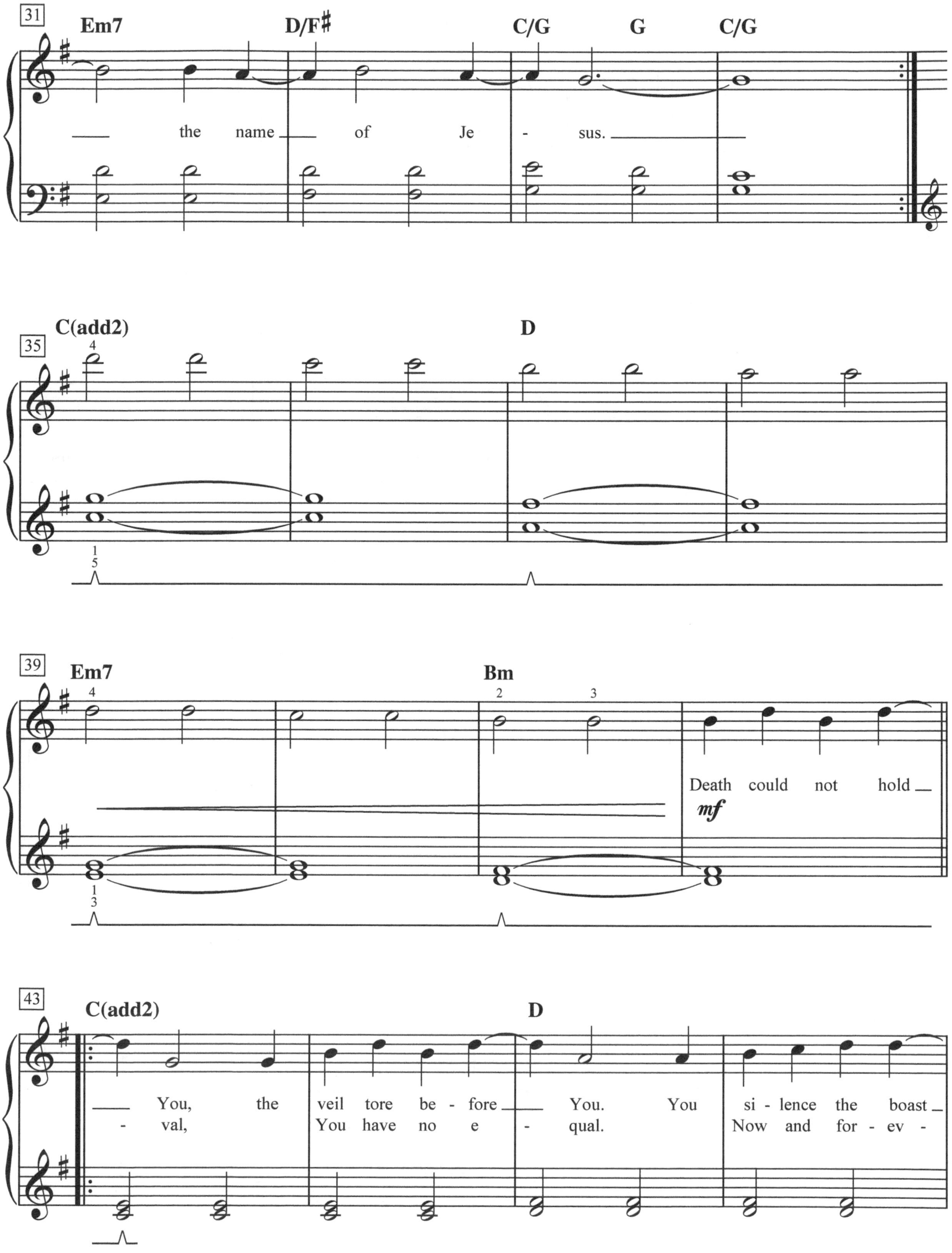
31
Em7
D/F♯
C/G
G
C/G
the name of Je - sus.
35
C(add2)
D
39
Em7
Bm
Death could not hold
mf
43
C(add2)
D
You, the veil tore be - fore You. You si - lence the boast
- val, You have no e - qual. Now and for - ev -

47
Em7
Bm7
of sin and grave. The heav - ens are roar -
- er, God, You reign. Yours is the king -
51
C(add2)
D
- ing the praise of Your glo - ry, for You are raised
- dom, Yours is the glo - ry, Yours is the name
55
Bm7
1.
D
to life a - gain. You have no ri -
a - bove all
2.
59
D
G
names. What a pow-er-ful name it is, what a pow-er-ful name it is,
f

63
D/F♯
Em7
D/F♯
the name of Je - sus Christ, my King.
67
C/G
G
What a pow-er-ful name it is,
noth-ing can stand a - gainst.
71
D/F♯
Em7
D/F♯
What a pow-er-ful name it is, the name of Je -
75
C/G
G
C/G
C(add2)
- sus.
rit.
p

WHO YOU SAY I AM

Words and Music by REUBEN MORGAN
and BEN FIELDING
Arranged by Phillip Keveren

11
Am G F C
love for me! Who the Son sets free, oh, is
15
G Am G F
free in - deed. I'm a child of God, yes, I
19
1. 2.
C C
am. am. In my
23
G
Fa - ther's house there's a place for me. I'm a

27
Am G F C
child of God, yes, I am. I am
31
Am G/B C
cho - sen, not for - sak - en. I am who You say I am.
34
F Am G/B
You are for me, not a - gainst me. I
37
C F C
am who I say I am. Who the Son sets

40
G
free, ___ oh, is free in - deed. ___ I'm a
43
Am G F C
child of God, yes, I am. In my
47
G
Fa - ther's house ___ there's a place for
50
Am G F C
me. ___ I'm a child of God, yes, I am. ___

THE PHILLIP KEVEREN SERIES

PIANO SOLO

00156644 **ABBA for Classical Piano** $15.99
00311024 **Above All** $12.99
00311348 **Americana** $12.99
00198473 **Bach Meets Jazz** $14.99
00313594 **Bacharach and David** $15.99
00306412 **The Beatles** $19.99
00312189 **The Beatles for Classical Piano** $17.99
00275876 **The Beatles – Recital Suites** $19.99
00312546 **Best Piano Solos** $15.99
00156601 **Blessings** $14.99
00198656 **Blues Classics** $14.99
00284359 **Broadway Songs with a Classical Flair** $14.99
00310669 **Broadway's Best** $16.99
00312106 **Canzone Italiana** $12.99
00280848 **Carpenters** $17.99
00310629 **A Celtic Christmas** $14.99
00310549 **The Celtic Collection** $14.99
00280571 **Celtic Songs with a Classical Flair** $12.99
00263362 **Charlie Brown Favorites** $14.99
00312190 **Christmas at the Movies** $15.99
00294754 **Christmas Carols with a Classical Flair** $12.99
00311414 **Christmas Medleys** $14.99
00236669 **Christmas Praise Hymns** $12.99
00233788 **Christmas Songs for Classical Piano** $14.99
00311769 **Christmas Worship Medleys** $14.99
00310607 **Cinema Classics** $15.99
00301857 **Circles** $10.99
00311101 **Classic Wedding Songs** $12.99
00311292 **Classical Folk** $10.95
00311083 **Classical Jazz** $14.99
00137779 **Coldplay for Classical Piano** $16.99
00311103 **Contemporary Wedding Songs** $12.99
00348788 **Country Songs with a Classical Flair** $14.99
00249097 **Disney Recital Suites** $17.99
00311754 **Disney Songs for Classical Piano** $17.99
00241379 **Disney Songs for Ragtime Piano** $17.99
00364812 **The Essential Hymn Anthology** $34.99
00311881 **Favorite Wedding Songs** $14.99
00315974 **Fiddlin' at the Piano** $12.99
00311811 **The Film Score Collection** $15.99
00269408 **Folksongs with a Classical Flair** $12.99
00144353 **The Gershwin Collection** $14.99
00233789 **Golden Scores** $14.99
00144351 **Gospel Greats** $14.99
00183566 **The Great American Songbook** $14.99
00312084 **The Great Melodies** $14.99
00311157 **Great Standards** $14.99
00171621 **A Grown-Up Christmas List** $14.99
00311071 **The Hymn Collection** $14.99
00311349 **Hymn Medleys** $14.99
00280705 **Hymns in a Celtic Style** $14.99
00269407 **Hymns with a Classical Flair** $14.99
00311249 **Hymns with a Touch of Jazz** $14.99
00310905 **I Could Sing of Your Love Forever** $16.99
00310762 **Jingle Jazz** $15.99
00175310 **Billy Joel for Classical Piano** $16.99
00126449 **Elton John for Classical Piano** $19.99
00310839 **Let Freedom Ring!** $12.99
00238988 **Andrew Lloyd Webber Piano Songbook** $14.99
00313227 **Andrew Lloyd Webber Solos** $17.99
00313523 **Mancini Magic** $16.99
00312113 **More Disney Songs for Classical Piano** $16.99
00311295 **Motown Hits** $14.99
00300640 **Piano Calm** $12.99
00339131 **Piano Calm: Christmas** $14.99
00346009 **Piano Calm: Prayer** $14.99
00306870 **Piazzolla Tangos** $17.99
00386709 **Praise and Worship for Classical Piano** $14.99
00156645 **Queen for Classical Piano** $17.99
00310755 **Richard Rodgers Classics** $17.99
00289545 **Scottish Songs** $12.99
00119403 **The Sound of Music** $16.99
00311978 **The Spirituals Collection** $12.99
00366023 **So Far...** $14.99
00210445 **Star Wars** $16.99
00224738 **Symphonic Hymns for Piano** $14.99
00366022 **Three-Minute Encores** $16.99
00279673 **Tin Pan Alley** $12.99
00312112 **Treasured Hymns for Classical Piano** $15.99
00144926 **The Twelve Keys of Christmas** $14.99
00278486 **The Who for Classical Piano** $16.99
00294036 **Worship with a Touch of Jazz** $14.99
00311911 **Yuletide Jazz** $19.99

EASY PIANO

00210401 **Adele for Easy Classical Piano** $17.99
00310610 **African-American Spirituals** $12.99
00218244 **The Beatles for Easy Classical Piano** $14.99
00218387 **Catchy Songs for Piano** $12.99
00310973 **Celtic Dreams** $12.99
00233686 **Christmas Carols for Easy Classical Piano** $14.99
00311126 **Christmas Pops** $16.99
00368199 **Christmas Reflections** $14.99
00311548 **Classic Pop/Rock Hits** $14.99
00310769 **A Classical Christmas** $14.99
00310975 **Classical Movie Themes** $12.99
00144352 **Disney Songs for Easy Classical Piano** $14.99
00311093 **Early Rock 'n' Roll** $14.99
00311997 **Easy Worship Medleys** $14.99
00289547 **Duke Ellington** $14.99
00160297 **Folksongs for Easy Classical Piano** $12.99
00110374 **George Gershwin Classics** $14.99
00310805 **Gospel Treasures** $14.99
00306821 **Vince Guaraldi Collection** $19.99
00160294 **Hymns for Easy Classical Piano** $14.99
00310798 **Immortal Hymns** $12.99
00311294 **Jazz Standards** $12.99
00355474 **Living Hope** $14.99
00310744 **Love Songs** $14.99
00233740 **The Most Beautiful Songs for Easy Classical Piano** $12.99
00220036 **Pop Ballads** $14.99
00311406 **Pop Gems of the 1950s** $12.95
00233739 **Pop Standards for Easy Classical Piano** $12.99
00102887 **A Ragtime Christmas** $12.99
00311293 **Ragtime Classics** $14.99
00312028 **Santa Swings** $14.99
00233688 **Songs from Childhood for Easy Classical Piano** $12.99
00103258 **Songs of Inspiration** $14.99
00310840 **Sweet Land of Liberty** $12.99
00126450 **10,000 Reasons** $16.99
00310712 **Timeless Praise** $14.99
00311086 **TV Themes** $14.99
00310717 **21 Great Classics** $14.99
00160076 **Waltzes & Polkas for Easy Classical Piano** $12.99
00145342 **Weekly Worship** $17.99

BIG-NOTE PIANO

00310838 **Children's Favorite Movie Songs** $14.99
00346000 **Christmas Movie Magic** $12.99
00277368 **Classical Favorites** $12.99
00277370 **Disney Favorites** $14.99
00310888 **Joy to the World** $12.99
00310908 **The Nutcracker** $12.99
00277371 **Star Wars** $16.99

BEGINNING PIANO SOLOS

00311202 **Awesome God** $14.99
00310837 **Christian Children's Favorites** $14.99
00311117 **Christmas Traditions** $10.99
00311250 **Easy Hymns** $12.99
00102710 **Everlasting God** $10.99
00311403 **Jazzy Tunes** $10.95
00310822 **Kids' Favorites** $12.99
00367778 **A Magical Christmas** $14.99
00338175 **Silly Songs for Kids** $9.99

PIANO DUET

00126452 **The Christmas Variations** $14.99
00362562 **Classic Piano Duets** $14.99
00311350 **Classical Theme Duets** $12.99
00295099 **Gospel Duets** $12.99
00311544 **Hymn Duets** $14.99
00311203 **Praise & Worship Duets** $14.99
00294755 **Sacred Christmas Duets** $14.99
00119405 **Star Wars** $16.99
00253545 **Worship Songs for Two** $12.99

Prices, contents, and availability subject to change without notice.